STUPID EASY INVESTING

TO GENERATE

PASSIVE INCOME

TABLE OF CONTENTS

INTRODUCTION 6

CHAPTER TWO - GETTING STARTED WITH INVESTING IN THE STOCK MARKET 8

    2.1 IDENTIFYING YOUR PERSONAL 9
    APPROACH TO INVESTING 9
        2.1.1 TIME HORIZON 10
        2.1.2 NET WORTH 11
    2.2 RISK TOLERANCE 12
    2.3 DIVIDENDS 14

CHAPTER THREE - INVESTING IN MUTUAL AND INDEX FUNDS 15

    3.1 INDEX FUNDS 15
    3.2 MUTUAL FUNDS 17
    3.3 A BORING INVESTMENT IN INDEX FUNDS THAT WILL MAKE YOU RICH IN 50 YEARS 18
    3.4 MUTUAL FUNDS OR INDEX FUNDS 19

CHAPTER FOUR - UNDERSTANDING THE 21

STOCK MARKET 21

    4.1 UTILITIES STOCKS 22
    4.2 FINANCE STOCKS 24
    4.3 CONSUMER DISCRETIONARY STOCKS 25

4.4 CONSUMER STAPLES 27
4.5 HEALTHCARE 28
4.6 ENERGY 30
4.7 INDUSTRIALS 31
4.8 TECHNOLOGY 33
4.9 TELECOMMUNICATIONS 35
4.10 MATERIALS 37
4.11 REAL ESTATE 38

CONCLUSION 41

To My Wife,

You Are the Health of My Soul

DISCLAIMER

None of the information in this book is meant to be used as financial advice, and is only meant for informational purposes. Any opinions that are expressed in this book is personal to the author and the author makes no guarantee of any kind regarding the fullness of any information or analysis provided.

The author will not be responsible for any loss arising from investment decisions based on a perceived recommendation derived from the contents of this book. Invest only after acknowledging and accepting the risks at your own discretion.

INTRODUCTION

Investing has become much more accessible to the average person due to the advent of low-commission investment platforms such as Robinhood, Fidelity, and TD Ameritrade. This has thus led to a significant influx of new investors into the stock markets.

Investing can be regarded as a way of allowing your money to work for you and the financial world today offers a plethora of asset classes that you can potentially invest in, from stocks, to index funds, to mutual funds. As a result, many new investors find it difficult to decide on which asset they should invest in.

In this book, you will be provided with an overview of the different characteristics of each asset class. Each type of asset will also be evaluated for its potential profitability with regards to both current and future market conditions.

Before we proceed, I would like to put out a disclaimer that I am biased towards making an investment in index funds that most people would consider to be "boring".

By the time you have finished reading this book, I believe that you will understand the reasons behind my preferred investment approach. Without further ado, let's get started.

CHAPTER TWO

GETTING STARTED WITH INVESTING IN THE STOCK MARKET

To begin, one must first comprehend what investing entails and how it may assist ordinary people in benefiting from the growth of the economy. The concept behind investing is to put a portion of your money into financial products such as stocks, bonds, mutual funds, commodities, and real estate.

This is done in the hopes of increasing the value of these assets as they continue to grow and profit. It also serves another role in addition to generating money from your assets.

By putting your money to work rather than keeping it in the bank, you will be better able to counteract the depreciating effects of inflation on your money. Investments in each of these financial product categories are typically undertaken with distinct objectives in mind.

Some financial products are riskier but provide a larger chance of higher returns, while others are less risky but offer a lower but more consistent yield. The amount of cash you have, your eventual objective of investing, and your general financial stability, which limits the amount of risk you can accept, will all influence your investment approach. As a result, this portion of the book will focus on presenting the various asset classes and giving you all the information that you need to make informed investment decisions.

2.1 IDENTIFYING YOUR PERSONAL APPROACH TO INVESTING

Knowing what sort of investor you are can help you to pick the proper investments to make so that you are both comfortable with the level of risk you are taking and satisfied with the amount of profit that you are making. There are three main types of investors.

People who are comfortable with high levels of risk and are willing invest in less established assets in exchange for a chance of earning bigger returns would make up the first category of investors. The second group would like more stable investments, which are the polar opposite of the first. The third group would place themselves in the center, with a portfolio that includes a mix of higher-risk and lower-risk assets.

2.1.1 TIME HORIZON

Before you can place yourself in one of these categories, you must first decide what your investment time horizon is. Your time horizon as an investor is the amount of time that you intend to hold your assets before selling them. An individual investing with the objective of saving for a down payment on a house, for example, may have a two- to three-year time horizon. An individual investing for retirement, on the other hand, may have a time horizon of twenty to thirty years. The time horizon of an individual will determine whether a more cautious or riskier portfolio will put him or her in the best position to achieve the largest amount of profit.

After you have determined your financial objectives, you may assess the amount of time that you will be able to retain your assets without having to make withdrawals. People with longer time horizons, such as those saving for retirement, may want to take on more risky assets.

This is because, over time, their assets will be able to recover from any economic downturns and will enjoy price appreciation alongside the world's continuously growing economy as technology improvements and population expansion enhance economic output.

Short-term investors, such as those who are saving for a house, vehicle, or college tuition, will be less risk tolerant and will be more comfortable with more conservative choices. This protects individuals from being too negatively impacted by a bad economic cycle while also allowing them to potentially make a decent profit on their investment.

2.1.2 NET WORTH

Your net worth will be another key aspect that you should evaluate. To calculate your net worth, take the value of all assets you own minus obligations such as credit card debt. Individuals with a higher net worth will have higher risk capitals, which refers to the amount of money that each person may lose without negatively impacting their present lifestyle.

As a result, they will be able to take on higher-risk ventures without the fear of losing money. Investors with lower risk capitals, on the other hand, would be wise to invest in safer financial products such as index funds or bonds.

Although existing assets typically influence future investing decisions, there are numerous other factors at play, such as age and salary. These factors might allow investors with traditionally low risk capitals to take on more risk.

For example, a freshly graduated student with promising job prospects will be able to maintain higher risk investments in his portfolio despite having a low initial risk capital and net worth since he is confident that he will be paid a consistent and steady wage and will have little or no obligations.

2.2 RISK TOLERANCE

After knowing which levels of risk you are comfortable with, you can categorize yourself as having an aggressive, moderate, or low risk tolerance. This is where various investment techniques will be implemented. Investors that are ready to invest in more volatile financial assets, such as equities, are known as aggressive investors.

Riskier activities, such as buying options contracts or shares of smaller companies, might result in either a huge loss or a large profit. As a result, such investors will need to make a commitment to knowing more about the global economy and markets.

Individual business stocks are frequently researched by reading financial reports, evaluating indicators, and closely tracking the company's developments. With each investment, you will be able to make better informed judgments. Overall, ambitious investors will have to go above and beyond to gather as much information as possible in their quest for maximum profits while simultaneously taking on the greatest risk.

Moderate investors are individuals who are ready to take on a small amount of risk in exchange for a small increase in profits. A moderate portfolio usually consists of a combination of mutual funds, shares of established companies, and bonds that will provide positive returns over a lengthy period of time. Most long-term investors favor moderate-risk assets that outperform the market thanks to compound interest. The objective of such investments is often to establish a retirement fund through regular savings.

For example, if one saves $1,000 each year, after 30 years, the sum will have grown to over $100,000 at a 7% annual growth rate.

Conservative investors are cautious of risk and are more inclined to invest with the sole purpose of beating yearly inflation rates than growing their wealth. As a result, liquid assets with a high level of security and stability will be favored.

They would probably put their money into bank certificates of deposit, money market funds, or bonds. These investments are chosen by people with a short time horizon or those who are retired and just want to retain the nest egg they have accumulated during their lifetime.

Although returns will be smaller, at approximately 2% to 3% per year, investments in this category are quite stable and will not be susceptible to the volatility that may be found in other assets such as equities.

2.3 DIVIDENDS

Dividends from a company refers to the distribution of its earnings to its shareholders. This means that as long as you own shares of a dividend-paying company, you may receive a payout in either cash or additional stock.

You can then either treat the dividends as a source of passive income or you can also choose to reinvest your dividends. With a sufficiently large investment, you can potentially live off dividend incomes that are typically paid out on a quarterly basis.

However, there are certain types of stocks that do not pay out dividends, and those are considered to be growth stocks, where investors derive most of the value of being an investor through price appreciation.

CHAPTER THREE

INVESTING IN MUTUAL AND INDEX FUNDS

Investing in mutual and index funds is a highly popular investment method due to its passivity and its advantage of offering diversification. When you make an investment in either a mutual or index fund, you are essentially letting a professional manage and invest your money for you.

In this chapter, we will be discussing the pros and cons of mutual and index funds. Following that, a comparison between the returns that you may potentially generate from investing in these two types of financial entities will be made.

3.1 INDEX FUNDS

Index funds are one of the most popular stock market investment financial instruments. They can be regarded as a portfolio that tracks the performance of a diverse set of businesses. This gives investors a wide variety of market exposure that is automatically diversified, lowering volatility while allowing profits to be realized when the index rises as a whole. Index funds are the preferred investing option for retirees since they do not need to be actively managed and serve as a relatively hands-off financial asset.

The S&P 500 index fund, which is listed on the New York Stock Exchange and comprises 500 of the biggest businesses in the United States, is an example of an index fund. As a result, investors may effectively invest in the whole U.S. economy and benefit as the economy expands year after year due to increased productivity.

There is a plethora of index funds that follow various components of the market. The Dow Jones Industrial Average is a stock market index that monitors the performance of 30 large-cap businesses in the United States, including Apple (AAPL), Boeing Co. (BA), and McDonald's Corp. (MCD). There are also riskier index funds that invest in firms that are more likely to expand, appealing to a wider spectrum of investors.

If you choose to invest in index funds, you will also benefit from earning a dividend income. This means that you can potentially set up a healthy stream of passive income through investing in index funds.

To summarize, index funds offer diversity that protects investors from single-company misfortunes while still providing excellent long-term returns.

3.2 MUTUAL FUNDS

Mutual funds are professionally managed investment funds that manages money that is pooled together from various entities. The total sum of money of each fund is then managed and invested as a singular entity. Similar to index funds, they offer the benefits of diversification.

However, the key difference between mutual funds and index funds lies in the fees and expenses involved. Investors typically have to pay a much higher fee to invest in mutual funds as these funds are actively managed.

This means that for an investor to obtain the same return on investment, the mutual fund will have to be extremely adept at making excellent investment choices. Similar to index funds, mutual funds may generate dividends depending on the types of stocks included in the fund.

There are many types of mutual funds available on the market, with each focusing on a specific subset of the overall stock market. For example, some mutual funds may choose to specialize in investing in certain countries, while other funds may choose to specialize in certain industries.

3.3 A BORING INVESTMENT IN INDEX FUNDS THAT WILL MAKE YOU RICH IN 50 YEARS

Let us consider a scenario where you invest $10,000 in index fund X. If the index fund grows at 10% in that year, you would have $11,000 at the end of the year. Assuming a consistent rate of growth at 10% annually, your initial $10,000 investment would grow to $1,173,908 after 50 years.

If you expanded the period of investment, the original investment would have grown to $3,044,816 and $7,897,469 after 60 and 70 years respectively.

These numbers may seem shocking, and it is only made possible due to the power of compounding returns which facilitates exponential growth. You may think that such consistent returns are non-existent in the market and are too good to be true. You may then be surprised to learn that the S&P500 has successfully returned 10.24% per year, on average, since 1960.

Keep in mind that the returns quoted above are not factoring the possibility of you making regular contributions to add towards your initial investment. If you make regular contributions, the compounding effect will lead to your portfolio being significantly larger. In addition, these numbers do not account for the dividend payouts that are historically set at between 3% and 5% for the S&P500.

Even while keeping your money invested, you could be generating passive income to sustain your lifestyle. This is why I personally believe in investing in boring index funds like the S&P500 that will simply make you rich if you are willing to be patient.

While index funds may not outperform the general market in the short-term, they have historically been successful in performing better than the overall stock market in the long-term.

3.4 MUTUAL FUNDS OR INDEX FUNDS

At this point in time, you may be wondering whether you should invest in a mutual fund or an index fund. To begin, let us first understand how much of an impact the fees of a mutual fund would have on overall returns. To illustrate, consider a $1,000 investment in a mutual fund that has a management fee of 0.82% that will be charged each year.

At 7% annual returns over 30 years, the initial $1,000 investment would have grown to about $86,000, with a total of about

$15,000 in fees incurred. However, if the same returns were achieved with an index fund with a management fee of 0.09%, the initial investment of $1,000 would have grown to $99,000 at the end of 30 years.

The situation as described above shows that a mutual fund will have to perform much better than an index fund in order for investors to enjoy the same overall rates of returns. While this is possible, a majority of mutual funds underperform the S&P500 index after factoring in management fees.

To illustrate how rare this is, only 24 mutual funds outperformed the S&P 500 over a seven-year period out of 123 total funds in the Investment Association's North American sector.

To conclude, it is definitely possible for you to find a mutual fund that can outperform the market. However, it will be difficult for you to do so and the odds are stacked against you with under 20% of mutual funds being successful in this endeavor. As such, my overall conclusion is that investing in index funds may be safer and more effective.

CHAPTER FOUR

UNDERSTANDING THE STOCK MARKET

When investing in the stock market, it is imperative that you understand the characteristics and properties of each sector. For example, sectors like utilities are likely to perform much better in economic downturns, while the industrials sector can be expected to perform better in more favorable economic conditions. The performance of equities is highly influenced by their finances and market performance.

As a result, investors should close attention to the news for the latest information on companies, which they may also acquire by reading earnings reports, product updates, mergers and acquisitions news, and so on.

There are many different types of stocks in many industries, each with its own volatility and indicators. There are 11 primary sectors that make up the stock market.

By understanding the different sectors of the stock market, you may potentially be able to capitalize on shifts in market conditions to take up new profitable positions in your portfolio.

4.1 UTILITIES STOCKS

Electric, gas, and water businesses make up the utilities sector, which offers services that are critical to the broader economy. Dividend-paying stocks in this category generate consistent income from the company's profits and are among the least volatile types of equities available.

This is due to government regulation of the utility industry, which bans firms from generating excessive profits at the expense of customers. The government does, however, guarantee profits to a certain level so that businesses may continue to operate in a sustainable manner.

Long-term investors that want to generate income from their assets through dividend distributions choose utility equities. Utility equities give out higher-than-average dividend yields, with an annual industry average of over 3%.

Stocks in this industry, on the other hand, are less likely to appreciate rapidly since growth and earnings are controlled. NRG Energy, CenterPoint Energy, NextEra Energy, and others are reputable companies in this field.

Interest rates and the overall condition of the economy are important indicators for the utilities business. As utility infrastructure generally requires high levels planning and capital, only firms large enough to reap sufficient economies of scale to operate profitably will exist.

These companies are often part of oligopolies or monopolies where they are either the sole or one of the few possible providers in a market. Companies may take out loans to finance infrastructure improvements and maintenance, and so interest rates will have a direct impact on utility companies' finances.

During economic downturns, investors regard the utilities industry as a safe haven. Utilities are essential services, and their revenues are unlikely to be affected by economic downturns.

Furthermore, amid a terrible economic climate, interest rates are likely to be cut to stimulate the economy, which would benefit utility companies even more. As a result, utilities are the best business to invest in when the economy is still recovering, and they are also a good choice for moderate and conservative investors who are investing for the long-term.

4.2 FINANCE STOCKS

Banks, investment funds, insurance businesses, and real estate corporations make up the financial industry. This category includes firms and individuals who provide loans, insurance, and financial services.

Retail and commercial banking, asset management, payment processing, and accounting are among the services provided by financial institutions. Citigroup, Bank of America, and JPMorgan Chase are examples of the large established firms in this sector.

Investors in finance stocks generally receive income in the form of dividends from their after-tax profits. This is done when the firm has excess cash after reinvesting a percentage of its profits in R&D, acquisitions, and operating expenditures.

As a result, finance stocks are in great demand as low-risk investments since financial firms are less likely to collapse and can provide income, low volatility, and even stock value appreciation.

The function of financial institutions is inextricably connected to the overall performance of the economy. This is because a robust economy will result in more corporate loans for investments and more consumer spending, resulting in more borrowing and hence higher profits on interest rates imposed by banks on those loans.

In conclusion, the financial industry is a great investment since it has historically produced consistent yearly returns and is regarded one of the most fail-resistant businesses in the world.

4.3 CONSUMER DISCRETIONARY STOCKS

This group of equities will include well-known firms that supply consumer products to the economy. In this sector, you may find media firms, clothing companies, and phone makers.

Consumer discretionary stocks come in many forms, and they do well when the economy is robust and consumer spending is high. Apple (AAPL), Disney (DIS), McDonalds (MCD), and Amazon (AMZN) are all well-known firms in this field.

Investments in this sector are typically undertaken when the economy is rebounding from a bad economic cycle or when the economy is strong and salaries are high, resulting in greater consumer spending. Consumer discretionary equities have been shown to outperform the stock market as a whole throughout a healthy market cycle.

However, they tend to underperform the average stock during economic downturns and recessions. GDP growth, inflation, interest rates, and the economy's overall health are the key indicators to watch while contemplating an investment in this industry. High GDP growth indicates greater spending by businesses and consumers, indicating that the economy is in good shape.

As a result, customer preferences tend to favor higher-end items, resulting in increased income for these enterprises. Moderate inflation may also suggest reasonable levels of consumer expenditure, implying healthy sales and profitability. Deflation, on the other hand, frequently encourages saving and advises minimal expenditure, resulting in reduced spending on consumer discretionary items.

Interest rates will also be a key economic indicator, as low interest rates stimulate spending on big-ticket products, while high interest rates encourage spending on low-ticket items.

To sum up, during economic recoveries and booms, investors would do well to invest in consumer discretionary companies since they will be able to benefit from increased consumer spending.

During worse economic cycles, investors may choose to avoid this category of equities in favor of more recession-resistant stocks. Long-term investors with a higher risk tolerance hold a bigger share of these companies since they have the potential to generate high returns.

In the ten years after the crisis in 2008, the consumer discretionary sector has increased 224.82 percent in value as a total, compared to the S&P500 index's 94.51 percent growth.

4.4 CONSUMER STAPLES

Consumer staples companies are not to be mistaken with consumer discretionary companies because, while both rely on the sale of products used in the typical person's everyday life, one focuses on necessities and the other on normal and luxury items. Food and beverage firms, as well as grocery chains, make up the consumer staples industry. Procter & Gamble (P&G), Kimberly-Clark (KMB), and Tyson Foods (TSN) are all well-known firms in this industry.

This industry's equities usually appreciate at a slower rate than the broader stock market, and they are favored by conservative investors who want equities that are less volatile. Companies in this industry are known for paying out large dividends to shareholders, making them a suitable addition to any portfolio looking for a regular source of income.

Consumer staples companies regularly outperformed other industries during recessions, since customers are unable to avoid purchasing essentials like food, water, and personal hygiene items. As a result, they're an important part of a portfolio's defensive strategy against worse business cycles.

GDP growth and the health of the labor market are two indicators for investors to evaluate. Workers in the country will likely earn lower salaries as a result of reduced GDP growth and a weaker job market, and some may even be laid off.

As a result, the typical worker's pay will decrease, and consumer spending will decrease across the economy. The consumer staples sector, on the other hand, will be protected from demand declines since demand for essentials will likely remain consistent across all rates of economic growth, allowing businesses to remain practically untouched. In conclusion, an investor should diversify into consumer staples equities to provide adequate protection against economic downturns while also producing a sizable income from the high dividend yields.

4.5 HEALTHCARE

Healthcare is constituted by biotechnology, hospitals, and pharmaceutical firms. The companies are typically diversified and offer a variety of services, including medication distribution, medical device distribution, insurance, and research.

Healthcare has a large budget in almost every economy, and it is always necessary regardless of the economic environment. As a result, healthcare is typically seen as a stable sector.

However, when economies weaken, individuals may be less inclined to spend on healthcare. Furthermore, governments and research organizations may become less eager to support innovative medication and procedure development, stifling the expansion of healthcare businesses.

Healthcare firms usually fare better in aging countries, as demand for healthcare items rises as the immune systems of the elderly deteriorate. Investments in the healthcare business are undertaken in order to increase returns and diversify portfolios. As medical technology advances, the likelihood of discovering cures and treatments increases, resulting in increased profits.

Although healthcare expenditure is projected to fall in weaker economies, healthcare companies still outperform the stock market on average because spending on medications and hospital care is not likely to fall as rapidly as other services that are deemed a need.

Overall, it is a complicated sector whose performance will be determined through the evaluation of a series of factors.

Biotechnology firms, whose performance is frequently dependent on breakthroughs and research achievements, are a good fit for moderate and aggressive investors, while cautious investors might consider adding hospital and service provider stocks to their portfolio. Johnson & Johnson (JNJ), and Biogen (BIIB) are a few examples of large-cap healthcare companies.

4.6 ENERGY

Oil, gas, refinery, and power businesses make up the energy industry. Energy equities are highly reliant on crude oil and natural gas prices, and they are frequently vulnerable to market volatility as a result of global geopolitical shifts.

Stocks in this category can yield significant profits, but they also carry a high amount of risk. Price changes are frequently influenced by a slew of unforeseen and uncontrollable factors, which can result in big gains or losses.

Making a successful oil strike and discovering a large oil resource, for example, will almost certainly result in a significant increase in the value of the oil firm that discovered the field. Oil production agreements and contracts will be the primary determinants of global oil supply, affecting a company's income and profitability. Accidental oil spills or fires, which are prevalent in the sector, can result in substantial stock value losses.

For example, when the British Petroleum Company (BP) released five billion barrels of oil into the Gulf of Mexico, it resulted in fatalities and pollution, as well as significant financial losses for its stockholders. Oil production and exploration are frequently connected to quickly changing global politics.

When Russia refused to reduce oil output in the face of declining oil prices in 2020, Saudi Arabia declared a price war and increased production, causing oil prices to plummet.

Following the pricing war, the value of energy businesses around the world plummeted dramatically.

As a result, the energy industry has the potential to provide high profits, but it is also vulnerable to tensions and disputes among major economies. You should only invest in the energy sector after thorough study into the target company's long-term viability and the general state of international relations.

Investing in this category without proper study would be nothing more than gambling, in which your money is put at risk in exchange for the chance of big returns. The bulk of shareholders in energy firms are well-informed aggressive investors.

4.7 INDUSTRIALS

Aerospace, defense, machinery, construction, and manufacturing companies make up the industrial sector. The performance of these businesses is heavily linked to the state of the economy.

Construction businesses are more likely to win more government and private contracts in a robust economy, which need the assistance of the industrial sector.

Expanding economies are also more likely to spend substantially on infrastructure in order to promote economic growth, which will assist this industry. Companies, on the other hand, tend to underperform during recessions because demand for industrial items falls rapidly.

Because economies are impacted by global political and macroeconomic developments, industrial stocks are considered volatile. If investments are made when the economy emerges from a recession and manufacturing picks up quickly, the returns from this sector can be substantial.

On the contrary, when the economy begins to stagnate and decline, they will be one of the most impacted industries.

Since a result, speculative transactions will have a significant negative impact on the value of the firms, as investors frequently react to recession worries by withdrawing their cash from industrial equities.

Apart from being a high-risk, high-reward asset, they are also viewed as a good source of income since the firms are typically able to generate a strong and steady cash flow, allowing for substantial dividends for shareholders.

The prospect of large profits created by firms in this area attracts both aggressive and moderate investors, who are advised to consider a long-term investment. Boeing (BA) and Caterpillar (CAT) are two examples of large-cap industrial corporations (CAT).

4.8 TECHNOLOGY

With firms like Microsoft (MSFT), Apple (AAPL), and Amazon (AMZN) being valued at trillions of dollars, technology stocks have become one of the most attractive industries to invest in. Over the last five years, the technology sector has outperformed the stock market by a wide margin. The majority of technology businesses are growth stocks, which are bought because of their proclivity for quick expansion and growth. Electronics, software, artificial intelligence, computer science, and social media are all areas in which companies in this industry operate.

Companies in this field have a proclivity for exploding in popularity and growing at breakneck speeds. As a result, it is not uncommon to see stocks like Advanced Micro Devices (AMD) provide investors with returns of more than 1,500 percent over the past ten years.

Most big technology firms contributed significantly to the development of the products that we use on a daily basis. Apple (APPL), Nvidia (NVDA), and Google (GOOG) are among them.

As most firms' market valuation is predicated on future growth expectations, the tech industry can be extremely volatile. Technology develops swiftly and may be adopted by the masses in a matter of weeks, which means that investments are often speculative, and share prices fluctuate rapidly as new discoveries are made public.

Zoom, a video-conferencing platform, is an excellent illustration of this phenomena. In December 2019, they had just over 10 million daily users on their site. Covid-19 has expanded to over 200 million daily participants by March 2020, demonstrating a demand for a solution for office professionals to work successfully from home.

Their stock price has more than quadrupled since December of last year.

Following the advent of tech behemoths such as Facebook and Google, the tech industry has outperformed the stock market to a large extent, making it one of the most attractive sectors for new investors to put their money in.

Traditional investment principles do not apply to technology firms, which have considerably higher than normal profit-to-earnings ratios, and some may even be losing money. Growth is frequently pushed at the price of sustainability and profitability.

Hence, investing in this industry should be done with prudence since the returns on investment might be quite high, but they can also collapse as quickly as rivals or disruptors arise. Furthermore, newer businesses may overspend in order to speed up the growth process, which can lead to them running out of funds and eventually collapsing.

Aggressive investors' portfolios are usually dominated by technology equities. A safer bet would be to buy shares in more established businesses like Apple, which have built a solid business strategy and a devoted customer base while also sitting on a big pile of cash, allowing them to expand while staying capable of innovating and weathering any economic downturns.

Many investors are attracted to acquiring shares of firms that are undertaking an Initial Public Offering (IPO), in which equities are first issued and sold on the stock market for the first time. Although tremendous gains can be achieved, as shown with the IPO of Beyond Meat (BYND), the outcomes can also be disastrous, as seen with the IPO of Uber Technologies (UBER).

4.9 TELECOMMUNICATIONS

Cable, internet, and satellite businesses are all part of the telecom industry. As the financial barriers to entry are high, these are generally larger businesses that own significant market shares. Telecom companies have a history of strong growth rates and little to no competition.

In recent years however, the sector is experiencing intense competition and must adapt fast in order to remain competitive and profitable. While calls and cable services used to be the primary source of revenue, the focus has changed to providing high-speed internet, secure communication connections, and data transmission.

Share prices in this sector can be extremely unpredictable, and they can plummet fast during a slump. However, telecommunications equities have also had long-term success with investments from both cautious and aggressive investors.

Due to high hurdles to entry, conservative investors are drawn to major telecom operators that have built substantial infrastructure and have few to no competitors. These businesses are expected to generate a consistent stream of money from their clients, who are most likely on a subscription-based payment model. Larger businesses in this sector are more stable and will be able to weather adverse business conditions and competition.

As a result, conservative investors will prefer these shares that are less volatile and are able to provide a steady stream of income.

Aggressive investors may instead choose to invest in wireless communications firms, which often are tiny businesses with significant growth potential. Wireless communications have been highlighted as the only area where the telecom sector will be able to continue to thrive despite increased disruption in traditional telecom firms.

This will give investors with the best chances of making the most return on their investments. However, like with any investment in a smaller, yet-to-be-established company, there will be significant risks.

The typical tendency in telecom company market performance is that they outperform ordinary equities in a healthy economy and suffer significant price depreciation in weak markets.

As a result, investors are recommended to only consider long-term investments in this category of companies in order to minimize risks and avoid taking up too large of a position in the face of a sluggish and stagnating economy.

4.10 MATERIALS

Companies involved in mining, refining, and chemical processes make up the materials industry. The retrieval of raw resources, followed by processing and development to generate vital commodities for supply chains all over the world, is central to business strategies.

Oil, gold, stone, and rubber are some of the raw resources that are handled. The health of the economy will influence material demand as high consumption rates stimulate producers to boost production, which leads to a rise in material demand. Dupont de Nemours (DD), PPG Industries (PPG), and Exxon Mobil Corp. (XOM) are all well-known corporations in the materials sector.

As the success of these equities is so closely linked to the economy, GDP growth and interest rates are two economic indicators to keep an eye on. High GDP growth indicates that customers are spending more, resulting in manufacturers purchasing resources to increase supply levels.

As a result, the materials business will see a rise in profit and revenue. Lower loan rates would be advantageous to the sector as well. Low interest rates enable firms and individuals to borrow, resulting in increased spending and corporate infrastructure investment. Construction for both enterprises and homes will necessitate enormous quantities of raw materials, boosting industry demand and profitability.

4.11 REAL ESTATE

The real estate sector is made up of investments in various types of property, including residential, industrial, and retail. Companies generate revenue and profits by collecting rent on premises and increasing the value of their assets. You can invest in the real estate sector through Real Estate Investment

Trusts (REITs), each of which will come with a portfolio of real estate properties. Investors can purchase a share in commercial real estate holdings using these securities, and these portfolios include everything from hotels and healthcare facilities to office buildings and energy pipelines.

Real estate stocks often provide investors with a higher-than-average consistent supply of dividends from rental income, as well as the potential for long-term capital appreciation when property prices rise.

Because REITs are obligated by law to pay a substantial percentage of their revenues to investors, the dollar value of each share may only increase very slowly. As a result, real estate stocks are generally reserved for long-term investors looking for a steady stream of income.

American Tower (AMT), Crown Castle International (CCI), Prologis (PLD), and Equinix (EQIX) are the largest REITs in the United States (EQIX). Real estate companies may specialize across a wide range of property types.

For example, certain REITs may engage only in telecommunications property, while others may invest in data centers, retail, healthcare, and a variety of other buildings. The value of each of these property sectors will rise or fall depending on the advancements in that industry.

Real estate equities will be a very beneficial addition to long-term investors' portfolios if they are backed up by appropriate research.

CONCLUSION

Making effective investment choices sounds harder than it actually is. While you can optimize your portfolios through actively researching and reading up on the various financial products available in stock market, you are also able to simply invest in an index fund and get rich over the course of a few decades.

As briefly mentioned above, the power of compounding returns will allow you to enjoy exponential growth of your investments.

Hence, it is recommended that you start investing as soon as you can.

You can start by downloading an investing app such as TD Ameritrade, Fidelity, or Robinhood to get started with investing. A great index fund that you can look up is the Vanguard Total Stock Market Index Fund (VTI). VTI has returned an astounding 15.16% annually to investors over the 10 years, which makes it one of the best performing index funds out there. Dividend yields are set at about 2% annually, which will provide you with passive income on top of asset price appreciation.

With that, it is hoped that this book has provided you with a clear and succinct introduction to investing in the U.S. stock market, and has helped you to decide how you would want to invest your capital. I would then like to end this book off with a quote from investing legend Warren Buffet that could not be more apt.

"The stock market is a device for transferring money from the impatient to the patient". – Warren Buffet

www.ingramcontent.com/pod-product-compliance
Lightning Source LLC
Chambersburg PA
CBHW070140230526
45472CB00004B/1625